Vocabulary-Building
Graphic Organizers
& Mini-Lessons

by Judith Bauer Stamper

NEW YORK • TORONTO • LONDON • AUCKLAND • SYDNEY
MEXICO CITY • NEW DELHI • HONG KONG • BUENOS AIRES

Teaching Resources

Cover design by Maria Lilja
Interior design by Jeffrey Dorman
Illustrations by Dave Clegg

ISBN 0-439-54891-8
Copyright © 2006 by Judith Bauer Stamper
All rights reserved.
Printed in the USA.

1 2 3 4 5 6 7 8 9 10   40   12 11 10 09 08 07 06

Contents

Introduction

The power of words permeates every aspect of learning. A strong vocabulary builds strong readers, writers, speakers, and thinkers. Vocabulary understanding underlies students' reading comprehension—from a classroom science text about amphibians to an independent reading series like Harry Potter. A robust bank of words enriches students' writing by allowing them to express their thoughts with precision and liveliness. A vocabulary that they truly own and can use enables students to speak and think with confidence and effectiveness.

How can teachers motivate students of all levels to develop their vocabularies as well as their love of and curiosity about words? Graphic organizers provide a proven and invaluable teaching tool for vocabulary learning. For vocabulary instruction, a graphic organizer provides students with concrete, visual connections between words and their meanings. This book will help you and your students explore words and share the excitement of vocabulary growth.

What Is a Graphic Organizer?

A graphic organizer is a visual and graphic representation of relationships among ideas and concepts. This instructional tool comes in a variety of formats—from loose webs to structured grids—that help students process information they've gathered and organize their ideas (Bromley et al., 1995).

Graphic organizers make teaching and learning more rewarding. Visually appealing and accessible to both struggling and advanced students, graphic organizers help students to:

- connect prior knowledge to new information (Guastello, 2000);
- integrate language and thinking in an organized format (Bromley et al., 1995);
- increase comprehension and retention of text (Boyle & Weishaar, 1997; Chang, K. et al, 2002; Moore & Readence, 1984);
- organize writing (Ellis, 1994);
- engage in mid- to high levels of thinking along Bloom's Taxonomy (application, analysis, evaluation, and synthesis) (Dodge, 2005).

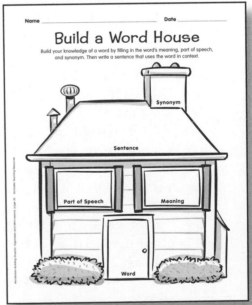

Goals of Vocabulary Instruction

The lessons and organizers in this book are designed to accomplish a number of strategic vocabulary goals:

Structural Analysis Understanding the underlying structure of the English language will give students the tools they need to tackle unfamiliar words and build a robust vocabulary. Students become empowered when they know the meaning of prefixes and suffixes and use them to understand multisyllabic words. A familiarity with word roots will lead to enhanced reading comprehension and success on standardized tests. Some of the lessons that teach structural analysis include:

- Root Word Tree (page 28)
- Prefix Piñata (page 32)
- Word Baseball (page 38)

Multiple Contexts Recognizing that context can provide clues to meaning will give students additional tools to comprehend unfamiliar words. Most important, students must learn to apply the meaning of a word to the context of their lives and truly own the word as part of their vocabularies. Some of the lessons that encourage students to use context are:

- Multiple Meaning Bug (page 14)
- Adjectives in Action (page 44)
- Homophone Hits (page 46)

Dictionary Skills Gaining practice using the dictionary will help students use this important word resource more effectively and with less trepidation. Some of the lessons that support dictionary usage include:

- Root Word Relay (page 30)
- Words That Count (page 34)
- Parts-of-Speech Snail (page 42)

Owning a Word Reaching the highest level of vocabulary knowledge—being able to define the word, apply it to a variety of contexts, and have it available for written and oral communication—is the real goal of vocabulary instruction. To accomplish this, students must use a word repeatedly in different contexts, including their own world. Some of the lessons that support this level of vocabulary understanding include:

- Word Jigsaw (page 16)
- Synonym Wheel (page 20)
- Build a Word House (page 24)

> One factor influencing the effectiveness of graphic organizers is the instructional context in which they are used. Studies suggest that to maximize the impact of graphic organizers on student learning, teachers need to state the purpose for using the organizer, model how to use it, and provide students with multiple opportunities for guided and independent practice and feedback.
>
> (National Center on Accessing the General Curriculum, 2002).

Using the Lessons and Graphic Organizers in This Book

The organizers can be used flexibly for a variety of learning situations for students in grades 4–6: whole class, small groups, and individual students. Use them as motivational graphic aids to teach and practice vocabulary skills and concepts.

Each lesson includes a skills focus, a statement of purpose, teaching suggestions, student samples, and a reproducible graphic organizer.

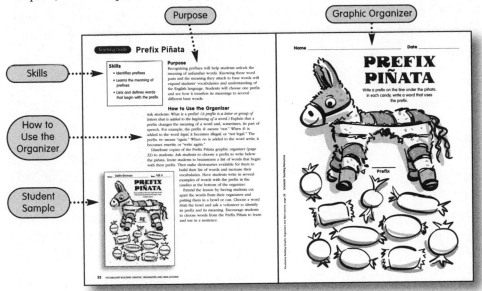

You can implement the organizers in any of the following ways:

- Draw the organizer on the board or on chart paper.
- Use the organizer as a template for an overhead transparency.
- Reproduce multiple copies of the organizer to pass out to students during class work.
- Have copies of the organizer available for students to use while working independently.

For whole-class instruction, use the lessons and the graphic organizers to model how to organize information visually. Invite students to offer ideas and suggest where this information would go in the organizer; this helps build background for their own independent or small-group work.

For small-group instruction, use the lessons and graphic organizers to provide students with the opportunity to work and learn cooperatively. When students are familiar with the format and purpose of an organizer, you can adapt it for use as a game or group activity. As students build background and brainstorm together, their learning is enriched by one another's experience.

For independent learning, use the graphic organizers to keep students engaged and focused on learning objectives. Once you've demonstrated how to complete the organizer, provide students with copies of the reproducible so they may complete their own during independent work time.

Use the lessons and graphic organizers in this book to help make vocabulary an exciting and successful part of your students' learning experience.

Word Web

Skills

- Explores different aspects of a content-area word

- Uses prior knowledge to build background about a word

- Makes connections with related words

Purpose

Word webbing is a strategy that builds on prior knowledge about a word and explores related words. Partners will choose a content-area word and fill out the web with related words. Working together on the web will pool students' prior knowledge and promote use of the word in their oral vocabulary.

How to Use the Organizer

Explain to students that one way to get to know a word is through word webbing. One word goes in the center of the web, and other words that relate to it come out from the center. Ask students: *What words can you think of that are related to the word* desert? *(Answers could include* cactus, rattlesnakes, tumbleweeds, sand, dry, *and* hot.*)*

Pair up students, then pass out a copy of the Word Web graphic organizer (page 9) to each pair. Instruct partners to choose a content-area word to write on the spider at the center of the web. It might be a math word like *geometry*, a geography word like *landforms*, or a science word like *skeleton*. Then have partners work together to fill in the word web with as many related words as possible.

More to Do

Group together two sets of partners to discuss their word webs. Have the new group members suggest more words for the web or ask questions about how their words relate to the word in the center.

Name ___Maria___   Date ___10/6___

Word Web

Write a content-area word on the spider. Then write other words on the web that are related to the first word.

representatives · vote · senators · laws · election · governor · Republican · Congress · government · White House · democrat · congressmen · primary · judges · president · soldiers · mayor

Word Web

Write a content-area word on the spider. Then write other words on
the web that are related to the first word.

Picture It!

Skills

- Identifies an unfamiliar word

- Uses a dictionary to find the meaning of the word

- Draws an image that illustrates the word, and writes a caption using the word

Purpose

Browsing a book for an unfamiliar word focuses students on individual words and challenges them to evaluate their vocabulary knowledge. After finding the meaning of their word in a dictionary, students will picture the word and use it in a caption sentence. This requires students to create both a visual and a written example of the word.

How to Use the Organizer

As students engage in independent reading, ask them to record any unfamiliar words that they might encounter. You might also read a challenging paragraph of a text or newspaper article and list the difficult vocabulary on the board.

Distribute copies of the Picture It! graphic organizer (page 11) to students. Ask students to write the vocabulary word they have chosen on the top of the organizer. Make dictionaries available for students to look up their words and jot down their meanings, plus any context sentences. Explain to students that a dictionary meaning is helpful, but that applying the meaning by using the word in a sentence is the real test of understanding a word.

Encourage students to come up with a visual representation of their word and draw the image on the graphic organizer. Then ask them to write a caption for their picture that uses the word and explains the image.

⭐ Picture It!

Choose a vocabulary word and write it at the top of the graphic organizer.
Then draw a picture to illustrate the word, and write a caption using the word.

Word _____

Caption _____

_____

Word Star

Skills

- Learns an unfamiliar word

- Uses a dictionary to find the word's part of speech, syllabication, synonyms, and antonyms

- Writes a meaningful sentence using the word

Purpose

Getting to know an unfamiliar word requires an understanding of its function as a part of speech, its relationship to other words, and its application in a meaningful sentence. Students will use the Word Star organizer to explore different aspects of a word and make it part of their own everyday vocabularies.

How to Use the Organizer

Begin by helping students brainstorm a list of unfamiliar words they want to incorporate into their vocabularies. Encourage students to look for "new" words in a fiction book, a content-area textbook, or a magazine or newspaper. List their words on the board.

Display a transparency copy of the Word Star graphic organizer (page 13) on an overhead projector. Choose a word on the list, and write it on the top of the star. Provide students with dictionaries, then enlist their help in finding the following information in a dictionary entry: syllabication, part of speech, synonyms, antonyms, and context sentences. As you find each piece of information for your chosen word, fill in the appropriate spaces in the graphic organizer.

Distribute copies of the Word Star graphic organizer and ask students to select one word on the list as their "word star" (a word other than the one you've already used). Have them write their chosen word at the top of the star and find the necessary information in their dictionaries.

More to Do

Review the words with the class by calling out a part of speech and asking for Word Stars that match it. Continue asking for more examples and information about the words.

Name Jeremy   Date 1/12

Word Star

Choose a word, then fill in the Word Star with information about your word.

Word
Essential

Syllables
Es-sential

Sentence
It is essential to walk your dog every day.

Synonyms
necessary

Part of Speech
Adjective

Antonyms
Needless

Word Star

Choose a word, then fill in the Word Star with information about your word.

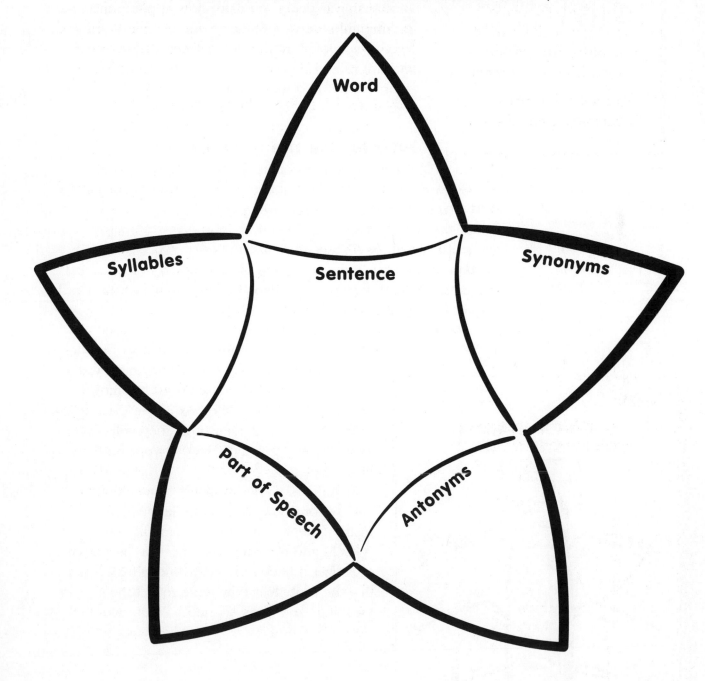

Word

Syllables

Sentence

Synonyms

Part of Speech

Antonyms

Multiple Meaning Bug

Skills

- Recognizes that a word can have several different meanings

- Identifies the part of speech of each meaning

- Uses the multiple meaning correctly in a context sentence

Purpose

Recognizing the multiple meanings of a word will help students develop a more complex and flexible vocabulary. Students will learn how to use a dictionary to determine the various meanings of a word and the correct parts of speech. They will use the various meanings in sentences to reinforce the word and to incorporate it into their written and spoken vocabularies.

How to Use the Organizer

Explain to students that many words have several different meanings. Write the following sentences on the board:

The young actor starred in his first <u>play</u>.

Do you want to <u>play</u> tennis?

Ask students: *In the first sentence, what part of speech is the word* play? (Noun) *What part of speech is the word in the second sentence? (Verb)* Ask students to explain the meaning of the word *play* in each sentence.

Have students brainstorm other words that have different meanings and list them on the board. Distribute copies of the Multiple Meaning Bug graphic organizer (page 15). Have students choose a word from the board and write it in the box above the bug's head. Explain to students that they will fill in two different meanings for the word on the bug's legs.

Make dictionaries available for students to check words and their multiple meanings. Instruct them to write each meaning, its part of speech, and a context sentence on the graphic organizer. Check students' work to make sure that the sentences they write reflect the correct meanings and parts of speech of the word.

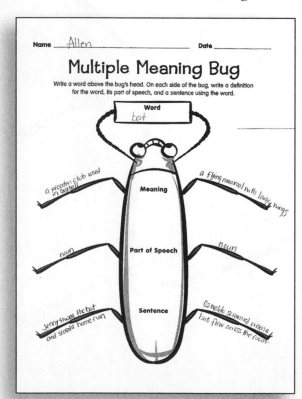

Multiple Meaning Bug

Write a word above the bug's head. On each side of the bug, write a definition for the word, its part of speech, and a sentence using the word.

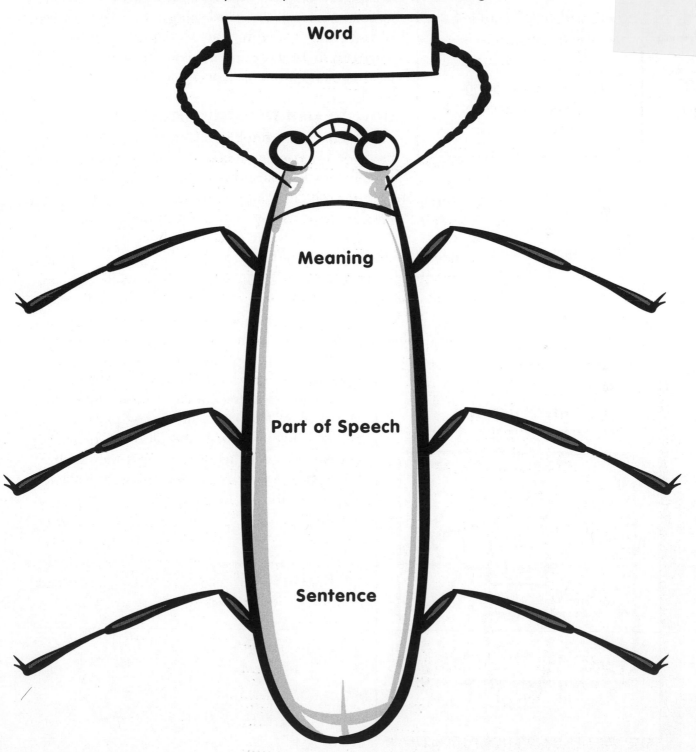

Word

Meaning

Part of Speech

Sentence

Word Jigsaw

Skills

- Explores an unfamiliar word

- Looks up the word in a dictionary

- Deepens understanding of the word by using it in different types of sentences

Purpose

As students fill out the Word Jigsaw graphic organizer, they will explore the meaning and use of an unfamiliar word. Students will practice using a dictionary to find the word's meaning and part of speech. They will apply the word's meaning by using the word in a sentence about themselves, in a question, and in an opinion.

How to Use the Organizer

The Word Jigsaw graphic organizer (page 17) can be used for any content area, but can be especially effective for language arts and social studies. For example, the word *protest* gains a deeper meaning for students when they apply it to themselves and use it in their opinions. Students could explore a word from a novel through the character it was used to refer to.

Distribute copies of the Word Jigsaw graphic organizer to students. Ask students to choose a word from their reading and write it at the center of the jigsaw puzzle. Next, have them explore what the word means by writing its definition from the dictionary and by using it in different sentences. Provide dictionaries for students to check the meanings of their words, then have them fill in the rest of the jigsaw pieces.

Let students color in the pieces of their jigsaw with crayons or markers if they wish. Post the jigsaw puzzles on classroom walls to share vocabulary knowledge.

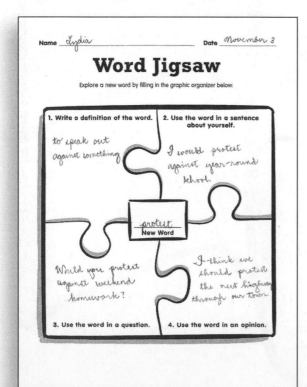

Name Lydia   Date November 3

Word Jigsaw

Explore a new word by filling in the graphic organizer below.

1. Write a definition of the word.
to speak out against something

2. Use the word in a sentence about yourself.
I would protest against year-round school.

protest
New Word

3. Use the word in a question.
Would you protest against weekend homework?

4. Use the word in an opinion.
I think we should protest the new highway through our town

Word Jigsaw

Explore a new word by filling in the graphic organizer below.

1. Write a definition of the word.

2. Use the word in a sentence about yourself.

_____
New Word

3. Use the word in a question.

4. Use the word in an opinion.

Antonym Examples

Skills

- Identifies two words that are antonyms, or have opposite meanings

- Looks up the words' meanings in a dictionary

- Applies knowledge of the words by using them in sentences

Purpose

Students will gain a deeper understanding of the meaning of antonyms by contrasting two antonyms on this graphic organizer. They will begin by writing the meanings of the words, then go deeper by writing example sentences. These concrete contexts will help define the words individually and in relation to each other. Context applications of the words help students understand the complexity of the words' meaning and their usefulness in everyday vocabularies. Working with a partner on the words helps enrich the words' meanings and transfers them to oral vocabulary.

How to Use the Organizer

As students read from a content-area textbook or a work of fiction, ask them to note down examples of antonyms that they encounter in their reading. Have students work individually or in pairs to select two opposite-meaning words that they want to study in depth.

Distribute copies of the Antonym Examples graphic organizer (page 19) to students. Instruct students to write the antonyms in the boxes on opposite sides of the organizer. Have them look up each word's definition in a dictionary and write it in the oval. Then ask them to write two sentences to demonstrate the meaning of each word. If necessary, model examples of antonyms, their meanings, and example sentences; or ask student volunteers to suggest examples.

Pair up students to share and discuss their antonyms, meanings, and example sentences.

Name ___Maria___ Date __12/13__

Antonym Examples

Pick two words that are antonyms and write them in the boxes. Next, write each word's definition and two sentences using each word.

meaning

the greatest possible amount

maximum

word

ANTONYM
ANTONYM

word

minimum

the smallest possible amount

meaning

The runner ran at maximum speed.
sentence

I will spend the maximum amount on sentence _my sister's gift._

He made minimum effort to study so
he failed sentence _the test._

A small plant will need minimum
water sentence

Antonym Examples

Pick two words that are antonyms and write them
in the boxes. Next, write each word's definition
and two sentences using each word.

meaning

word

sentence

sentence

word

meaning

sentence

sentence

ANTONYM
ANTONYM

Synonym Wheel

Skills

- Recognizes words that have similar meanings

- Identifies the difference in meaning between synonyms

- Builds vocabulary by associating words with similar meanings

Purpose

Identifying sets of synonyms will help students expand their vocabularies and use more complex words in place of common ones. Students will also recognize that words have shades of meaning, and they will learn which of two words with similar meanings best fits a certain context.

How to Use the Organizer

Ask students: *What are synonyms? (Words that have similar meanings)* Give the following examples: *big, enormous, huge, gigantic, colossal,* and *large*. Point out that even though synonyms have similar meanings, there are usually fine differences in meaning between synonyms. Ask students to describe the difference in meaning between the words *big* and *enormous* and to use each word in a sentence.

Distribute copies of the Synonym Wheel graphic organizer (page 21) to students. Invite students to choose a word to put in the middle of the wheel's hub. Then have them use a dictionary or thesaurus to look for synonyms of the word and write them in the spokes of the wheel. Finally, challenge students to differentiate the meanings of the synonyms by writing context sentences in the open spaces between the spokes of the wheel. Encourage students to use a dictionary to help them understand the subtleties among the synonym words.

More to Do

Post students' Synonym Wheels on a board in the classroom. Reinforce the words by naming a "hub" word and asking volunteers to give a synonym for it.

Synonym Wheel

Write a word at the center of the wheel. On each spoke, write a synonym of the word. Then write a sentence that uses the synonym correctly.

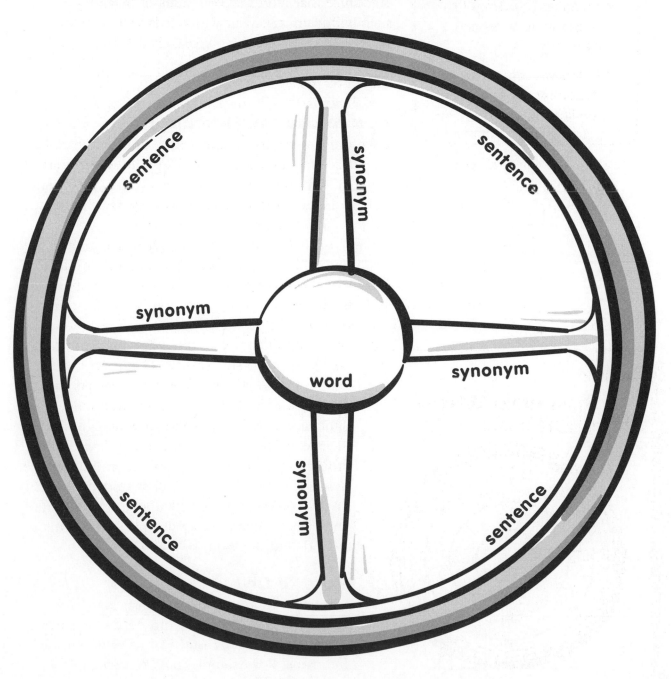

Target Word

Skills

- Explores different aspects of a word

- Looks up a word's meaning in a dictionary

- Identifies a word's synonyms, antonyms, and other related words

Purpose

Reading a dictionary's definition of a word is often not enough to know the word. To fully understand a new vocabulary word, students also need to know how other words relate to it. For example, what words have a similar meaning? What words mean the opposite thing? Using this graphic organizer, students define a word and identify its synonyms, antonyms, and other related words.

How to Use the Organizer

Make a transparency of the Target Word graphic organizer (page 23) and display it on an overhead projector. Write the word *cold* at the center of the bull's-eye and guide students to explore this simple word. Ask students: *What does* cold *mean? (Having a low temperature)* Write the definition in the circle around the center. Next, ask students to come up with words that have a similar meaning to *cold*, such as *freezing, cool, chilly*, and *icy*. Write these words in the third circle. Finally, challenge students to come up with words that mean the opposite of *cold*, such as *hot, burning, sizzling*, and *scorching*. Write these words on the outermost circle of the target.

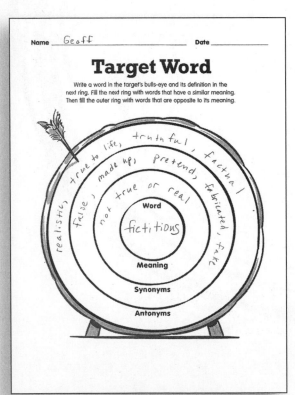

Distribute copies of the graphic organizer to students. Invite students to choose a word to explore. You may want to start them off with easy words or challenge them to use more difficult words, such as those they might find in their textbooks or independent reading books. Provide students with dictionaries and thesauruses to use for reference. Don't limit students to using single-word synonyms or antonyms for the outer rings. Encourage them to use phrases if it helps them define the word better.

More to Do

Another way to use the organizer is to have students write what the word describes and what it doesn't describe, instead of its synonyms and antonyms. For example, *cold* is *snow, ice, refrigerator, freezer*, or *winter*; *cold* is <u>not</u> the *desert, oven, sun*, or *fire*.

Target Word

Write a word in the target's bull's-eye and its definition in the next ring. Fill the next ring with words that have a similar meaning. Then fill the outer ring with words that are opposite to its meaning.

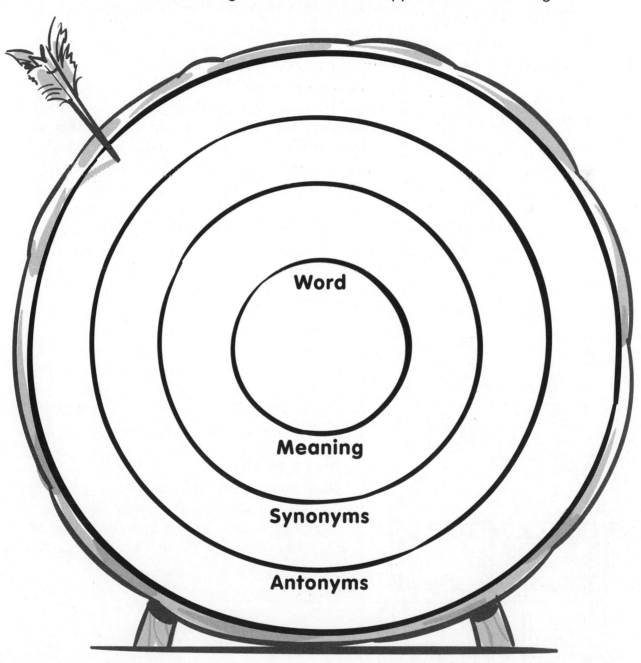

Word

Meaning

Synonyms

Antonyms

Build a Word House

Skills

- Explores the meaning of an unfamiliar, new vocabulary word

- Builds word meaning by identifying the word's definition, part of speech, and a synonym

- Uses the word in a context sentence

Purpose

Use the metaphor of parts of a house to help students understand the many facets of a word's meaning and usage. By filling in the graphic organizer, students will explore the parts of a word and how they add up to the whole meaning of the word.

How to Use the Organizer

Distribute copies of the Build a Word House graphic organizer (page 25) to students. Engage students in a discussion about how a word may be like a house. Explain that just as the door, windows, roof, and chimney show different aspects of a house, so do a word's definition, part of speech, synonym, and a context sentence show different facets of the word.

To use this graphic organizer, direct students to look for unfamiliar words from their science, math, or social studies lessons, or independent reading. Record the list of words on the board. Ask students to choose a word from the list and write it on the door of the Word House. Provide students with dictionaries and thesauruses to look up the meaning of the word, its part of speech, and a synonym. Students should fill in the graphic organizer as they find these pieces of information. Next, ask students to write a sentence, using the word in context.

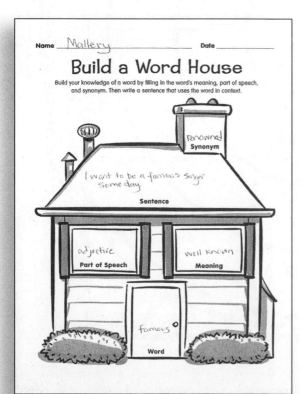

More to Do

Have students exchange papers with a partner and talk to each other about their Word Houses. Challenge students to write another sentence for their partner's Word House.

Build a Word House

Build your knowledge of a word by filling in the word's meaning, part of speech, and a synonym. Then write a sentence that uses the word in context.

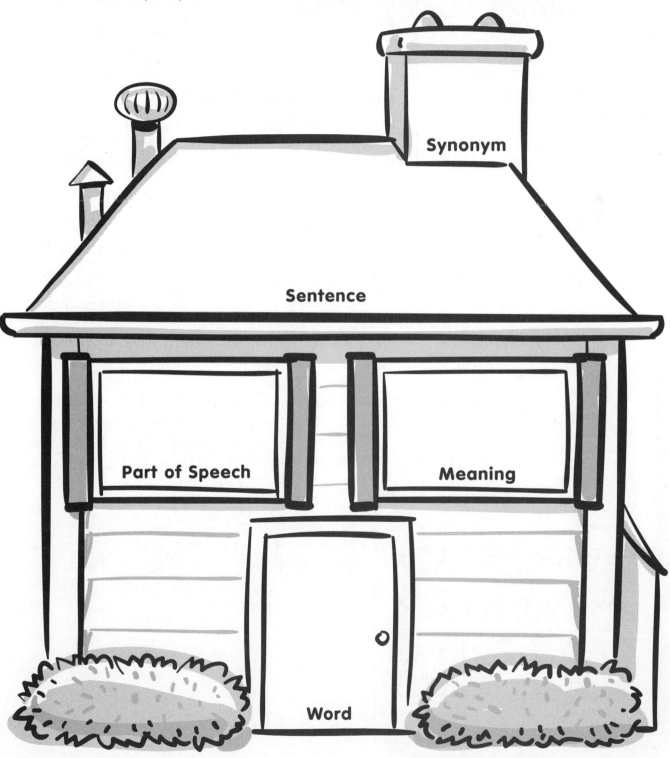

Synonym

Sentence

Part of Speech

Meaning

Word

Analogy Action

Skills

- Identifies relationships between words

- Creates analogies with a variety of relationships

- Completes a partner's analogies by recognizing the relationships between words

Purpose

Recognizing the relationship between two words and applying it to another word set encourages higher-order thinking about vocabulary. Students will use synonyms, antonyms, and part-to-whole relationships to create their analogies. They will also be practicing strategies that will prepare them for standardized test questions.

How to Use the Organizer

Explain to students that an analogy is a comparison that uses the relationship between two words as a pattern for another pair of words. Guide students to solve the following analogy:

sun is to moon as day is to ____.

Ask students: *What do you think is the relationship between the words* sun *and* moon? *(They're opposites.) What word do you think would fit in the blank? (Night)*

Explain to students that analogies can also show other kinds of relationships, such as synonyms and part-to-whole relationships. Ask students to give examples of synonyms and analogies using synonyms; for example, *difficult is to hard as simple is to easy.* Next, ask students to give examples of part-to-whole analogies, like *bat is to baseball as racquet is to tennis.*

Distribute copies of the Analogy Action graphic organizer (page 27) to students. Point out the different elements in the organizer. Explain that the two circles at the top are for synonyms, while the circle and square at the bottom are for antonyms. The middle of the organizer is for part-to-whole analogies. Have students fill in the organizer with an example of each kind of relationship. Remind them that the second pair of words should have the same relationship as the first pair of words.

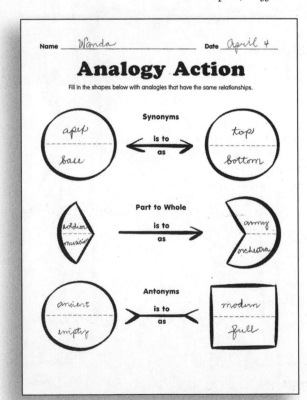

Analogy Action

Fill in the shapes below with analogies that have the same relationships.

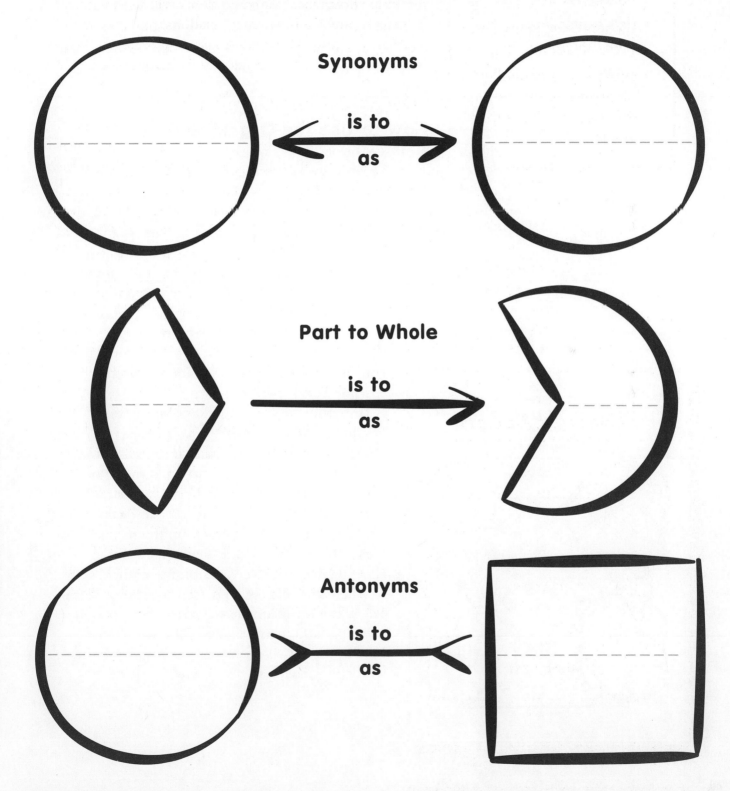

Synonyms

is to

as

Part to Whole

is to

as

Antonyms

is to

as

Root Word Tree

Skills

- Identifies common root words

- Lists examples of words from that root

- Relates the meaning of the words to their root

Purpose

Understanding how much of the English language is built on Latin and Greek roots will help students recognize unfamiliar academic words. Students will become familiar with common roots and explore words that are derived from them. While building their Root Word Tree, students will build their understanding of word origins and shared word meanings.

How to Use the Organizer

Write the word *inspector* on the board. Ask students: *What does this word mean? (A person who examines or inspects something)* Break the word apart by drawing lines after *in* and *spect*. Explain to students that many words consist of different parts called prefixes, roots, and suffixes. In the word *inspector*, the root is *spect*, which means "to see." Explain that a root is the core word part to which other parts are added; in this case, *in-* and *-or* are added to *spect*. Many roots in the English language come from Latin and Greek. A dictionary often gives the root that a word stems from. For example, the root *spect* comes from Latin.

Challenge students to think of other words that contain the root *spect*; for example, *prospect*, *spectator*, and *spectacles*.

Distribute copies of the Root Word Tree graphic organizer (page 29) to students. Together with the class, brainstorm a list of roots that students can use to build their Root Word Tree. Have students choose a root and write it at the base of the tree. Make dictionaries available for students to look up the meaning of their root and find words that come from it. Have them write the words on the branches.

When students have finished their Root Word Trees, call on volunteers to share their root, its meaning, and the meaning of the words that grow from it. Call on other students to use the words in sentences.

Root Word Tree

Write a root at the base of the tree. On the branches
write six or more words that use that root.

Root Word

Root Word Relay

Skills

- Identifies a root and its meaning

- Builds a list of words with that root

- Writes meaningful sentences using the words

Purpose

Recognizing roots is an important key to understanding the meaning of an unfamiliar word. Students will break a word into smaller parts, including its root. Knowing the meaning of common Greek and Latin roots can help student build a rich vocabulary, especially of academic and content words.

How to Use the Organizer

Explain to students that many words share a root, or word part that can be combined with other word parts to form words with common meanings. For example, the Latin root *equi* means "equal." Some words with this root are *equitable*, *equalize*, and *equality*.

Distribute copies of the Root Word Relay graphic organizer (page 31) to students. Tell students that they will be running a relay with a root and form words that contain it. When they complete four words from the root, they'll get across the finish line and win the race.

Have students write their root, its origin, and its meaning in the middle of the race track. Then have them go around the track, writing in words with the root, as well as meaningful sentences using the words. Make dictionaries available to help students build their word lists.

More to Do

Invite the class to play Root Word Relay together by working in teams of four. Call out a root and its meaning. Then challenge students to finish a relay race by naming words with that root.

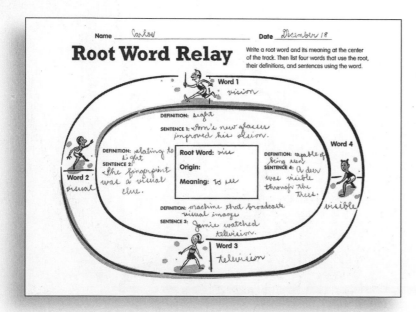

Name

Root Word Relay

Write a root word, its origin, and its meaning at the center of the track. Then list four words that use the root, their definitions, and sentences using the words.

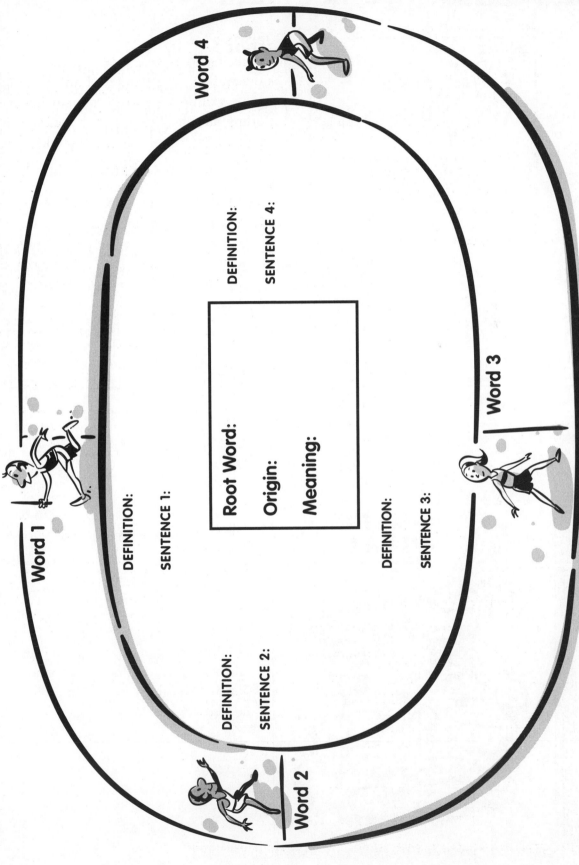

Word 1

DEFINITION:

SENTENCE 1:

Word 2

DEFINITION:

SENTENCE 2:

Word 3

DEFINITION:

SENTENCE 3:

Word 4

DEFINITION:

SENTENCE 4:

Root Word:

Origin:

Meaning:

Prefix Piñata

Purpose

Recognizing prefixes will help students unlock the meaning of unfamiliar words. Knowing these word parts and the meaning they attach to base words will expand students' vocabularies and understanding of the English language. Students will choose one prefix and see how it transfers its meanings to several different base words.

How to Use the Organizer

Ask students: *What is a prefix? (A prefix is a letter or group of letters added to the beginning of a word.)* Explain that a prefix changes the meaning of a word and sometimes its part of speech. For example, the prefix *il-* means "not." When *il-* is added to the word *legal*, it becomes *illegal*, or "not legal." The prefix *re-* means "again." When *re-* is added to the word *write*, it becomes *rewrite*, or "write again."

Distribute copies of the Prefix Piñata graphic organizer (page 33) to students. Ask students to choose a prefix to write below the piñata. Invite students to brainstorm a list of words that begin with their prefix. Then make dictionaries available for them to build their list of words and increase their vocabularies. Have students fill in several examples of words with the prefix in the candies at the bottom of the organizer.

More to Do

Extend the lesson by having students cut apart the words from their organizers and put them in a bowl or can. Choose a word from the bowl and ask a volunteer to identify its prefix and its meaning. Encourage students to choose words from the Prefix Piñata to learn and use in a sentence.

PREFIX PIÑATA

Write a prefix on the line under the piñata.
In each candy, write a word that uses
the prefix.

_____
Prefix

Words That Count

Skills

- Identifies number prefixes

- Uses number prefixes to recognize unfamiliar words

- Builds a word bank of words based on number prefixes

Purpose

Recognizing number prefixes can help students determine the meaning of an unfamiliar multisyllabic word. Students will learn to combine the meaning of the number prefixes with roots, suffixes, and other word parts to extrapolate the meaning of the whole word.

How to Use the Organizer

Explain to students that many words in our language are based on number prefixes. Write the words *bicycle* and *tricycle* on the board and ask students to define them. Then write *biplane* and *triangle* on the board and ask students to define them. Ask: *What do you think the prefix* bi- *means? (Two) What about the prefix* tri-? *(Three)* Challenge students to think of other prefixes that indicate numbers, such as *deca-, cent-, milli-,* and so on.

Distribute copies of the Words That Count graphic organizer (page 35) to students. Ask them to think of and write number prefixes in the first column. In the second column, have them write a word that uses each prefix. Next, have students write the word's definition in the third column. Encourage students to use their prior knowledge or a dictionary to fill out the chart, searching for unfamiliar examples to learn and then record their meanings.

Divide the class into six groups and assign each group one of the number roots. Have each group create a list or web of words beginning with the root and record their meanings. Post the results on a class bulletin board or wall.

Name Kerry   **Date** Feb. 11

Words That Count

Fill in the chart with number prefixes and words that use these prefixes.
Write the meaning of the words in the third column.

	Number Prefix/ Root	Word	Meaning
1	mono	monochromatic	having one color
2	bi	bilingual	speaking two languages
3	tri	tricycle	a vehicle with three wheels
4	quad	quarter	one-fourth of the whole
10	deca	decathlon	an event with ten events
100	centi	percent	part of one hundred

Words That Count

Fill in the chart with number prefixes and words that use these prefixes.
Write the meaning of the words in the third column.

1
2
3
4
10
100

Number Prefix/ Root	Word	Meaning

Suffix Machine

Skills

- Identifies suffixes
- Connects suffixes to base words
- Recognizes how a suffix changes a word's meaning and part of speech

Purpose

Learning about suffixes will help students understand how these word parts change a word's meaning and part of speech. Being able to recognize a suffix can help students read an unfamiliar word and comprehend its meaning. Suffixes are key to understanding how words in the English language are built from different word parts.

How to Use the Organizer

Write a list of common suffixes on the board, including -y, -tion, -ful, -ous, -ly. Explain to students that these are suffixes—letters or groups of letters that are added to the end of a word. Suffixes change the word's meaning and, often, its part of speech. Model the following example of adding a suffix to a word: *power + ful = powerful*. Ask students to use *power* and *powerful* in sentences. Point out that *power* is a noun; the suffix *-ful* changes it to *powerful*, an adjective. Challenge students to come up with words that end with the suffixes on the board.

Distribute copies of the Suffix Machine graphic organizer (page 37). Ask students to write three suffixes in the Suffix Machine. For each suffix, have students write a base word in the left column that, combined with the suffix, would produce a new word in the right column. Have students write the base word and new word's meaning and/or part of speech on the conveyor belt. As an additional challenge, have students write a sentence below the conveyor belts, using each word. Provide suggestions as necessary.

When students have completed their graphic organizers, call on volunteers to give examples of the suffix words they have created on the Suffix Machine. Challenge other students to use each word in a sentence and name its part of speech.

Suffix Machine

Write three suffixes on the screens in the machine. For each suffix, write a base word on the box at the left and the new word on the box at the right. Write each word's meaning and/or part of speech on the conveyor belt.

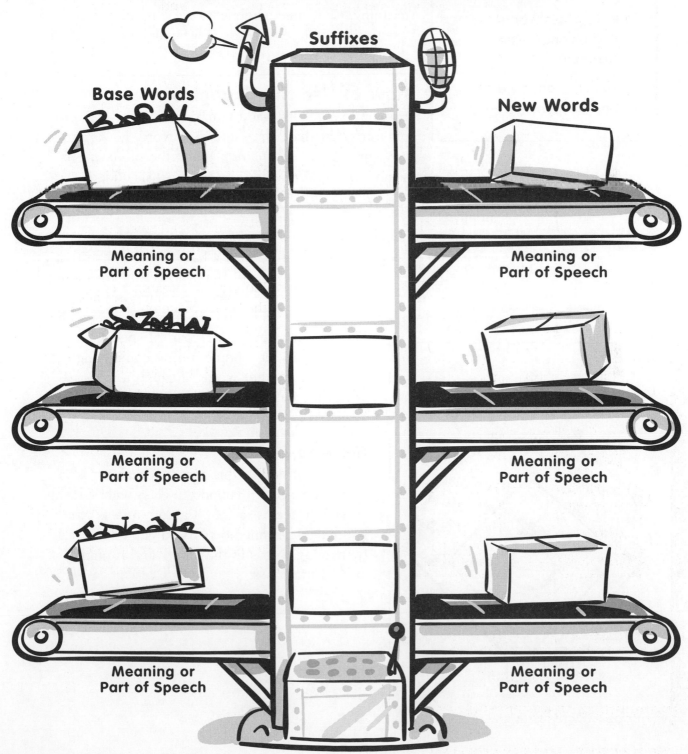

Word Baseball

Skills

- Adds prefixes and/or suffixes to a base word to create new words

- Recognizes words that belong to the same family

- Identifies each word's part of speech

Purpose

Recognizing the variation of words within the same family is a powerful means of building vocabulary. Prefixes, suffixes, and inflectional endings attached to a base word create different parts of speech and affect meaning. Challenge students to get a home run by writing four different words in a family and identifying their parts of speech.

How to Use the Organizer

Explain to students that a family of words is a group of words that share the same base word. For example, take the base word *popular*. When the prefix *un-* is added, it becomes *unpopular*. When the suffix *-ity* is added, *popular* becomes *popularity*. All three words belong to the same family.

Distribute copies of the Word Baseball graphic organizer (page 39) to students. Tell them to pick a base word and write it on the pitcher's mound. The goal is to "hit a homerun" by adding prefixes and/or suffixes to the base word and writing the new words between all the bases. As an extra challenge, have students identify each new word's part of speech. Students can hit a home run by completing the organizer; in other words, creating four words out of the base word. Make dictionaries available for students to build their words.

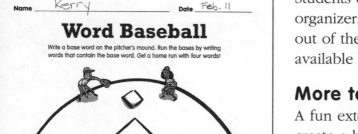

More to Do

A fun extension of this graphic organizer is to create a baseball diamond in class with students playing in teams of four. Call out a base word and have team members try to get a home run by naming words in the family and running around the bases.

Word Baseball

Write a base word on the pitcher's mound. Run the bases by writing words that contain the base word. Get a home run with four words!

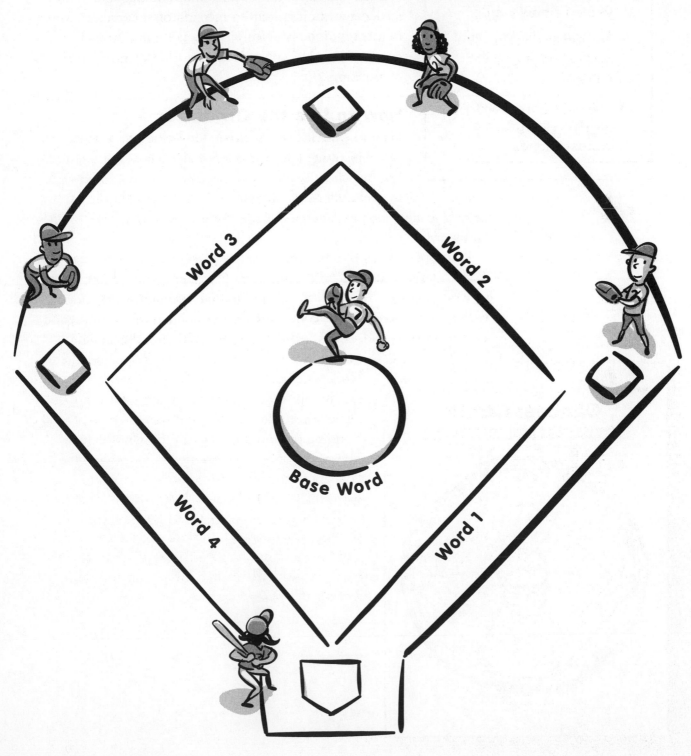

Word 3

Word 2

Base Word

Word 4

Word 1

Concept Circle

Skills

- Generates groups of words that belong to the same category

- Recognizes a word that doesn't belong to the category

- Identifies the category to which the group of words belongs

Purpose

Working with concept circles helps students build content-area vocabulary and identify the larger category of meaning that the words fall into. This organizer gives students an opportunity to recognize categories of words, to identify nonexamples of a category, and to make connections among words to find the shared category of meaning.

How to Use the Organizer

Remind students that words often belong to a larger category of meaning. In science class, for example, they learn a whole set of words when studying a topic such as ocean life. Ask students to brainstorm words that belong to that concept, such as *whale, shark, seaweed, coral, jellyfish,* and so on.

Distribute copies of the Concept Circle graphic organizer (page 41). Ask students to decide on a concept to fit in the middle circle, but <u>not</u> to write it in yet. Then tell them to fill in five sections of the pie with words that belong to that concept. Have them fill in the sixth section with a nonexample, or a word that doesn't belong to the category.

Have students exchange papers or assign pairs to work together.

Caution students to read all the words in the circle before determining the shared concept, and deciding on and crossing out the word that doesn't belong. Then instruct them to write the concept in the middle of the circle and add a sixth word that fits the concept. Ask partners to choose one of their concept circles to write on the board for the class to solve.

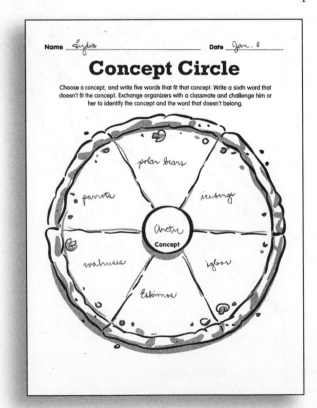

Concept Circle

Choose a concept and write five words that fit that concept. Write a sixth word that doesn't fit the concept. Exchange organizers with a classmate and challenge him or her to identify the concept and the word that doesn't belong.

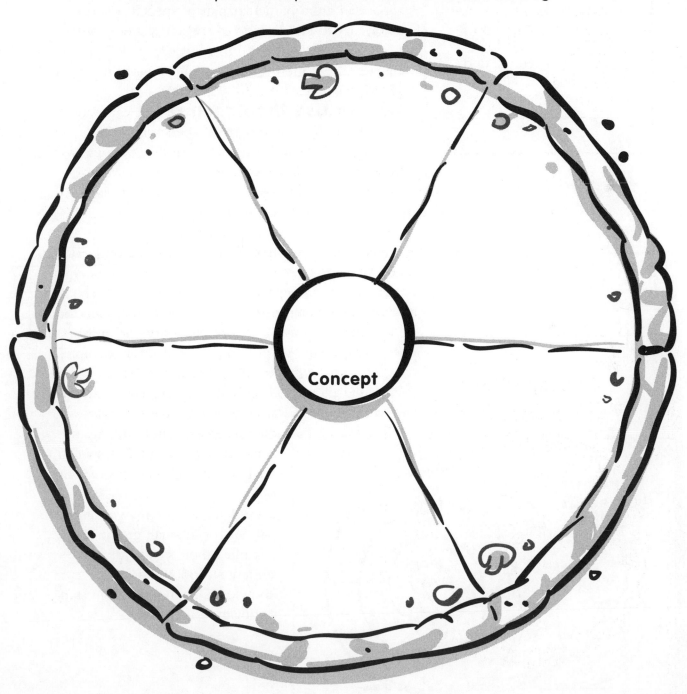

Concept

Parts-of-Speech Snail

Skills

- Reviews parts of speech

- Brainstorms vocabulary related to a concept or topic

- Identifies words that are nouns, verbs, and adjectives

Purpose

Recognizing a word's part of speech helps students know how to use the word in oral or written language. In this activity, students choose a general topic and then brainstorm words that both fit that topic and are a particular part of speech. Using a dictionary to check parts of speech will help students become acquainted with this dictionary skill and help them sharpen their understanding of word meaning.

How to Use the Organizer

Review the following parts of speech by asking students to define each one and provide examples:

- a **noun** names a person, place, or thing; for example, *pilot, community, robot*

- a **verb** shows action; for example, *jog, investigate, search*

- an **adjective** describes a noun; for example, *courageous, enormous, powerful*

Distribute copies of the Parts-of-Speech graphic organizer (page 43) to students. Explain that they will select a general topic and generate words related to that topic. Help students brainstorm broad topics to use in their Parts-of-Speech Snails; for example, *weather, transportation, math, sports*, and so on. Model examples of words for different parts of speech for the category of sports: noun, *umpire*; verb, *bounce*; adjective, *foul*. Have students complete the snail by filling in examples of each part of speech related to the chosen concept or topic.

Students will enjoy working with partners or in small groups to complete their snails. Allow students to pool their prior knowledge as they go from start to finish on their snails.

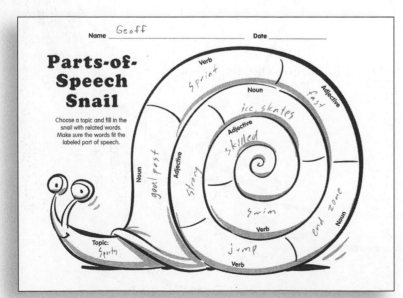

Name _____

Date _____

Parts-of-Speech Snail

Choose a topic and fill in the
snail with related words.
Make sure the words fit the
labeled part of speech.

Noun

Adjective

Verb

Verb

Noun

Adjective

Verb

Noun

Adjective

Topic:

Adjectives in Action

Skills

- Defines an adjective and identifies adjectives in text

- Uses adjectives to describe a fictional character

- Investigates the meaning of the adjectives by applying them to the character and to self

Purpose

Analyzing a fictional character through vocabulary will help sharpen students' knowledge of word meanings and give them tools for literature response. Applying the adjective to themselves will help transfer the words to their own experience and everyday vocabulary.

How to Use the Organizer

Begin by asking students: *What is an adjective? (A word that describes a noun)* Give students the following examples: *a smart girl, a tall boy, an adventurous man, a courageous woman.* For each example, ask students to identify the adjective. Then ask them to name a real person or fictional character who fits each of these adjective descriptions.

Distribute copies of the Adjectives in Action graphic organizer (page 45) to students. Have them think of a fictional character they have read about in class or in their independent reading. You might give examples like Harry Potter, Anne Shirley of Green Gables, Cam Jansen, or Homer Price. Direct students to write the name of the character in the first column and draw his or her picture.

In the next column, have students fill in three adjectives that describe the character. If they need help, ask them to think about things the character said or did. Then think about what adjectives would describe those actions or words. In the third column, have students provide evidence about why the adjective fits the character, and then use the adjective in a sentence describing the character. Finally, ask students to decide whether or not each adjective describes them as well and explain why or why not.

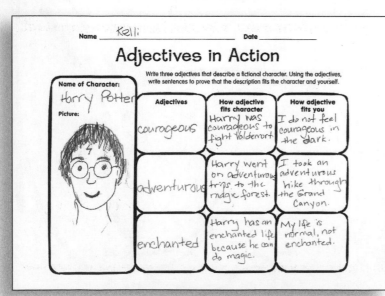

Adjectives in Action

Write three adjectives that describe a fictional character. Using the adjectives, write sentences to prove the description fits the character and perhaps yourself.

Adjectives	How adjective fits character	How adjective fits you

Name of Character:

Picture:

Homophone Hits

Skills

- Identifies homophones and their spellings

- Records pairs of homophones

- Uses the correct meanings of homophones in sentences

Purpose

Identifying homophone pairs and using each word in a sentence will help students distinguish their meanings and use the words correctly. Homophones are the cause of many spelling errors. Repeated use of the words in context will help students correctly choose which spelling to use.

How to Use the Organizer

Write the following sentences on the board:

The policeman _____ his whistle. The ocean is _____.

Read the first sentence aloud, inserting the word *blew* in place of the blank. Ask students to spell the word *blew*, and write it on the blank. Next, read the second sentence aloud, inserting the word *blue* in the blank. Again, ask students to spell the word and write it on the blank.

Explain to students that *blew* and *blue* are homophones—words that sound the same, but have different meanings and spellings. Challenge students to name other homophones and use them in sentences.

Distribute copies of the Homophone Hits graphic organizer (page 47). Ask students to brainstorm a pair of homophones and write them on the large notes in the organizer. Then have them write a meaningful sentence for each homophone that correctly uses its meaning in context.

More to Do

Play a game to reinforce the homophones. Call on a volunteer to name a homophone and read one of his or her context sentences. Ask other students to spell the homophone as it is used in the sentence. Assign points for correct answers.

Name _____

Homophone Hits

Fill in the notes with homophones.
Then write sentences that use the
homophones in the correct context.

Sentence 1: _____
_____

Sentence 2: _____
_____

Homophones

Bibliography

Bromley, K., L. Irwin-De Vitis, & M. Modlo. (1995). *Graphic Organizers: Visual Strategies for Active Learning*. New York: Scholastic Inc.

Boyle, J.R. & M. Weishaar. (1997). "The Effects of Expert-Generated Versus Student-Generated Cognitive Organizers on the Reading Comprehension of Students with Learning Disabilities." *Learning Disabilities Research and Practice*, 12(4), 228–235.

Chang, K.E., Y.T. Sung, & I.D. Chen. (2002). "The Effect of Concept Mapping to Enhance Text Comprehension and Summarization." *Journal of Experimental Education*, 71(1), 5–24.

Dodge, J. (2005). *Differentiation in Action*. New York: Scholastic Inc.

Ellis, E.S. (1994). "Integrating Writing Instruction with Content-Area Instruction: Part II: Writing Processes." *Intervention in School and Clinic*, 29(4), 219–230.

Guastello, E.F. (2000). "Concept Mapping Effects on Science Content Comprehension of Low-Achieving Inner-City Seventh Graders." *Remedial and Special Education*, 21(6), 356.

Moore, D. & J. Readence. (1984). "A Quantitative and Qualitative Review of Graphic Organizer Research." *Journal of Educational Research*, 78(1), 11–17.

National Center on Accessing the General Curriculum. (2002). http://www.cast.org/index.html